ACCA

Paper P5
Advanced Performance Management

Pocket notes

British library cataloguing-in-publication data

A catalogue record for this book is available from the British Library.

Published by:
Kaplan Publishing UK
Unit 2 The Business Centre
Molly Millars Lane
Wokingham
Berkshire
RG41 2QZ

ISBN 978-1-78415-720-3

© Kaplan Financial Limited, 2016

Printed and bound in Great Britain.

Contents

Exam guidance – keys to success in this paper

The aim of this paper is to apply relevant knowledge and skills and to exercise professional judgement in selecting and applying strategic management accounting techniques in different business contexts, and to contribute to the evaluation of the performance of an organisation and its strategic development. However it is important to remember that this paper is about application of techniques to real-life situations so you are expected not only to be able to describe and use a technique but to discuss implementation issues and the technique's usefulness in a particular scenario.

Paper P5 also has a strong relationship with Paper P3 Business Analysis in the areas of strategic planning and control and performance measurement and expects you to have your knowledge in place from paper F5 performance management.

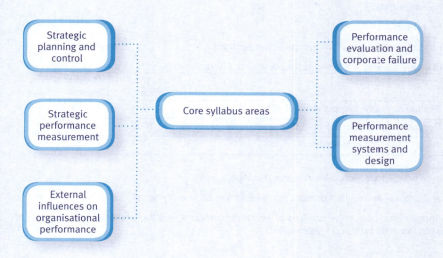

Strategic planning and control

Strategic performance measurement

External influences on organisational performance

Core syllabus areas

Performance evaluation and corporate failure

Performance measurement systems and design

The examination

The format

The examination paper will comprise two sections.

Total time allowed – 15 minutes reading and 3 hours writing.

		Marks per question	Number of marks
Section A	One compulsary question	50	50
Section B	Answer two from three questions	25	50
	Total marks		100

There will be four professional marks available.

Candidates will receive a present value table and an annuity table.

A range of topics may be covered in individual questions and the exam will contain a mix of computational and discursive elements.

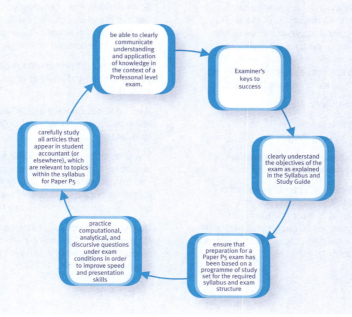

be able to clearly communicate understanding and application of knowledge in the context of a Professonal level exam.

Examiner's keys to success

clearly understand the objectives of the exam as explained in the Syllabus and Study Guide

ensure that preparation for a Paper P5 exam has been based on a programme of study set for the required syllabus and exam structure

practice computational, analytical, and discursive questions under exam conditions in order to improve speed and presentation skills

carefully study all articles that appear in student accountant (or elsewhere), which are relevant to topics within the syllabus for Paper P5

There will not always be a unique or correct solution to questions in Paper P5 examinations. Alternative solutions will be valid if they are supported by appropriate evidence and workings. Therefore if assumptions are made concerning a given scenario, they should be clearly stated.

Examination tips

Spend the first few minutes of the examination reading the paper.

Where you have a choice of questions, decide which ones you will do.

Divide the time you spend on questions in proportion to the marks on offer. One suggestion **for this examination** is to allocate 1.8 minutes to each mark available, so a 10-mark question should be completed in approximately 18 minutes.

Spend some time **planning** your answer. Stick to the question and **tailor your answer** to what you are asked. Pay particular attention to the verbs in the question.

Spend the last five minutes reading through your answers and making any additions or corrections.

If you **get completely stuck** with a question, leave space in your answer book and **return to it later**.

If you do not understand what a question is asking, state your assumptions. Even if you do not answer in precisely the way the examiner hoped, you should be given some credit, if your assumptions are reasonable.

Do everything you can to make things easy for the marker. The marker will find it easier to identify the points you have made if your answers are legible.

Key study tips

Ensure you review prior knowledge from earlier papers.

Revise the course as you work through it and leave sufficient time before the exam for final revision.

Cover the whole syllabus and pay attention to areas where your knowledge is weak.

Practice exam standard questions under timed conditions. Attempt all the different styles of questions you may be asked.

Read good newspapers and professional journals.

The examiner expects:

1. assumed knowledge to be in place
2. candidates to use the scenario
3. general business knowledge
4. a rounded view of the whole subject
5. candidates to be able to tackle calculations but the emphasis will not be on these
6. candidates to add value, for example by quantifying comments or discussing commercial implications
7. implications to be considered from a business manager's perspective.

Pass rates are still low. **The examiner recommends:**

1. using the scenario
2. avoiding question spotting
3. good time management – get the paper marked out of 100
4. answering the question asked
5. planning answers
6. that before the exam, students should study the whole syllabus, revise assumed knowledge and practice lots of past exam questions.

Quality and accuracy are of the utmost importance to us so if you spot an error in any of our products, please send an email to mykaplanreporting@kaplan.com with full details, or follow the link to the feedback form in MyKaplan.

Our Quality Co-ordinator will work with our technical team to verify the error and take action to ensure it is corrected in future editions.

1

Introduction to strategic management accounting

In this chapter

- Planning and control.
- The strategic planning process.
- The role of corporate planning.
- Critical success factors and key performance indicators.
- Long-term and short-term conflicts.
- The changing role of the management accountant.
- Strategic management accounting in multinational companies.
- Benchmarking.
- SWOT analysis.
- Gap analysis.

Exam focus

The emphasis of this section is on understanding the role of performance management in an organisation, to understand strategic management accounting and specific tools. It is important that, in addition to understanding the tools, you can also apply the tools to specific scenarios.

This section also explores the changing role of the management accountant and discusses contemporary issues and trends in performance management.

Planning and control

Definition

Strategic Planning is concerned with:

* where an organisation wants to be (usually expressed in terms of its objectives) and

* how it will get there (strategies)

Control is concerned with monitoring the achievement of objectives and suggesting corrective action.

The performance hierarchy

Characteristics of a mission statement:

Succint   Memorable   Enduring   A guide for employees to work towards the accomplishment of the mission   Addressed to a number of stakeholder groups

Strategic and operational planning and control

Strategic planning & control	Operational planning & control
Long-term, considering the whole organisation.	Short-term, based on a set of assets and resources.
Match activities to external environment and identify future requirements.	Rarely involves any major change.
High degree of uncertainty.	Unlikely to involve major elements of uncertainty.
Control by monitoring the strategy and how well objectives are achieved.	Will not lead to changes in strategy.

The strategic planning process

Strategic analysis

- External analysis to identify opportunities and threats.
- Internal analysis to identify strengths and weaknesses.
- Stakeholder analysis to identify key objectives and to assess power and interest of different groups.
- Gap analysis to identify the difference between desired and expected performance.

Strategic choice

- Strategies are required to 'close the gap'.
- Competitive strategy – for each business unit.
- Directions for growth – which markets/products should be invested in.
- Whether expansion should be achieved by organic growth, acquisition or some form of joint arrangement.

Strategic implementation

- Formulation of detailed plans and budgets.
- Target setting for KPIs.
- Monitoring and control.

The role of corporate planning

Definition

The term **corporate planning** refers to the formal process which facilitates the strategic planning framework described above.

> **Role of corporate planning in evaluating potential strategies**

Suitability
- Does the strategy have a strategic fit?

Acceptability
- Is the strategy acceptable to stakeholders?

Feasibility
- Can the necessary resources and competencies be.

- The results of the plans are compared against stated objectives.

- Action taken to remedy short falls in performance.

- This is an ongoing process.

Critical success factors and key performance indicators

Definition

Critical success factors (CSFs) are the vital areas where 'things must go right' for the business in order for them to achieve their strategic objectives. The achievement of CSFs should allow the organisation to cope better than rivals with any changes in the competitive environment.

Core competencies

Something that the organisation is able to do that is difficult for competitors to follow. The organisation will need to have the core competencies in place to achieve the CSFs.

Key performance indicators (KPIs)

The achievement of CSFs can be measured by establishing KPIs for each CSF and measuring actual performance against these KPIs.
KPIs are essential to strategy since **what gets measured gets done.**

Long-term and Short-term conflicts

Divisional autonomy – individual managers operate their business units as if they were independent businesses – seeking and exploiting local opportunities as they arise

Pressures on managers are for short-term results Strategy is concerned with the long-term

Potential for conflict

Rigid long-term plans can prevent the organisation responding to short-term opportunities or crises

Strict adherence to a strategy can limit creativity and flair

The adoption of corporate strategy requires that the interests of departments, activities and individuals are subordinate to the corporate interests

The changing role of the management accountant

ROLE OF MANAGEMENT ACCOUNTANT

Historically
- Role limted to implementation stage, e.g. responsible for operational budgeting and control.
- Focus is on internal factors and financial information.
- Focus is on the past.

Today
- Strategic role providing information on financial aspects of strategic planning e.g. competitors' costs.
- Uses internal and external information.
- Monitors performance in financial and non-financial terms.
- Focus is on the future.

Burns and Scapens studied how the role of the management accountant has changed over the last 20 years.

Driving forces for change:
- Technology.
- Management structure.
- Competition.

Leading to the following changes

- The role has changed from financial control to business support.
- The new role has been called a hybrid accountant.
- Accountants may no longer work in a separate accounting department.

Leading to the following benefits

- Accountants ensures strategic goals are reflected in performance management.
- Management accountant helps the strategic business unit to get the most from their information system.
- Management accountant can develop a range of performance measures to capture factors that will drive success.

The modern management accountant has a role in informing stakeholders of the financial and non-financial impact of the company's decisions.

A new approach to reporting is called integrated reporting. With integrated reporting one report captures the strategic and operational actions of management in its holistic approach to business and stakeholder wellbeing.

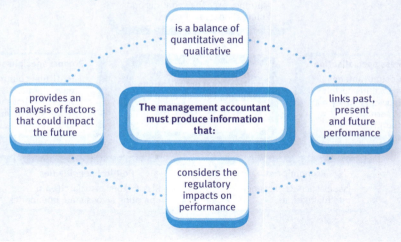

is a balance of quantitative and qualitative

provides an analysis of factors that could impact the future

The management accountant must produce information that:

links past, present and future performance

considers the regulatory impacts on performance

Strategic management accounting in multinational companies.

Administrative issues
- Impact on internal transactions of exchange rate movements, currency exchange controls and international tax treaties.

Process specialisation
- Cost advantages in locating certain types of activity in certain countries.

Key characteristics of multinational organisations requiring consideration by strategic management accounting

Product specialisation
- Particular countries have characteristic tastes that the multinational must cater to.

Economic risk
- Issues such as exchange rate fluctuations.

Political sensitivities
- Risk factors associated with operating across state boundaries.

Benchmarking

The objective of benchmarking is to understand and evaluate the current position of a business organisation in relation to best practice and to identify areas and means of performance improvement.

Types of benchmarking

Internal benchmarking

This is where another function or department of the organisation is used as the benchmark.

Competitor benchmarking

Uses a direct competitor in the same industry with the same or similar processes as the benchmark.

Process or activity

Focuses on a similar process in another company which is not a direct competitor.

Once the organisation has established which aspects of its performance should be benchmarked, it must establish metrics for these.

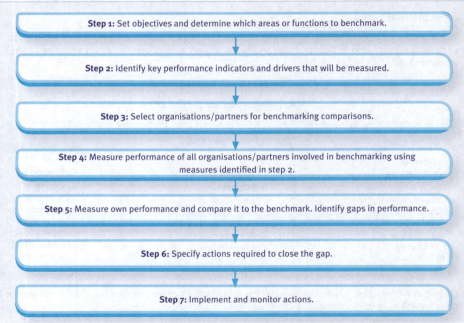

Step 1: Set objectives and determine which areas or functions to benchmark.

Step 2: Identify key performance indicators and drivers that will be measured.

Step 3: Select organisations/partners for benchmarking comparisons.

Step 4: Measure performance of all organisations/partners involved in benchmarking using measures identified in step 2.

Step 5: Measure own performance and compare it to the benchmark. Identify gaps in performance.

Step 6: Specify actions required to close the gap.

Step 7: Implement and monitor actions.

SWOT analysis (corporate appraisal)

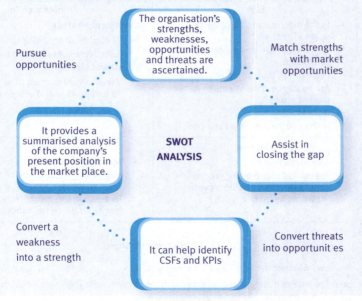

Pursue opportunities

The organisation's strengths, weaknesses, opportunities and threats are ascertained.

Match strengths with market opportunities

It provides a summarised analysis of the company's present position in the market place.

SWOT ANALYSIS

Assist in closing the gap

Convert a weakness into a strength

It can help identify CSFs and KPIs

Convert threats into opportunit es

Boston Consulting Group (BCG) matrix

		High Relative market share	Low Relative market share
Market growth	**High**	**Star** • Is the high reinvestment being spent effectively? • Is market share being gained, held or eroded? • Is customer perception improving? • Are customer CSFs changing as the market grows? • Net cash flow. • Is the star becoming a cash cow.	**Problem child** **Investment strategy** • Is market share being gained? • Effectiveness of promotional spend. **Divestment strategy** • Monitor contribution to see whether to exit quickly or divest slowly.
	Low	**Cash cow** • Net cash flow. • Is market share being eroded – could the cash cow be moving towards becoming a dog?	**Dog** • Monitor contribution to see whether to exit quickly or divest slowly. • Monitor market growth as an increase in the growth rate could justify retaining the product.

- the matrix shows whether the firm has a balanced portfolio.
- it can be used to assess business performance and performance management issues of an entity.

Exam focus

Exam sitting	Area examined	Question number	Number of marks
Sept/Dec 2015	CSFs	1(ii), (iii)	21
June 2015	Choice of metrics, SWOT	1(i), (iv)	26
December 2014	Benchmarking	1(iii)	16
June 2014	Mission	1(v)	6
December 2013	KPIs, CSFs and gap analysis	1(i)(iii)(iv)(v)	35
December 2012	Changing role of management accountant	5(a)	12
June 2012	Benchmarking	4	17
June 2012	KPIs	2(a)	12
December 2011	KPIs	2(a)	7
June 2011	BCG	4	20
December 2010	CSFs and KPIs	1(a)(c)	20
December 2010	KPIs	4(a)	4
December 2009	KPIs	2(b)(i)	12
December 2009	Mission, CSFs and KPIs	5	17

June 2008	Benchmarking	1(b)	7
December 2007	CSFs	3(b)	10
Pilot paper	Mission	2(a)(i)	5

2

Environmental influences

In this chapter

- External analysis.
- Stakeholders.
- Ethical issues.
- The impact of government policy.
- The impact of government regulation.
- Risk and uncertainty.

Exam focus

All organisations will be impacted by the environment in which they operate in and it is imperative that they consider the effect that factors such as risk, government regulation and social/ ethical issues will have on performance.

External analysis

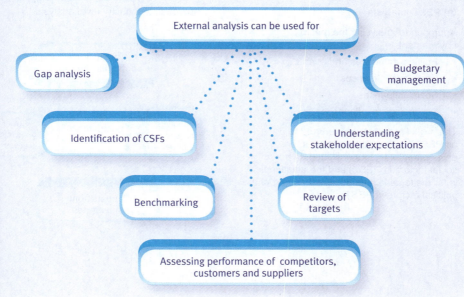

External analysis can be used for

Gap analysis

Budgetary management

Identification of CSFs

Understanding stakeholder expectations

Benchmarking

Review of targets

Assessing performance of competitors, customers and suppliers

Tools for external analysis

(a) PEST analysis

Approach to analysing the macro-environment:

- **P**olitical influences and events
- **E**conomic influences
- **S**ocial influences
- **T**echnological influences

The model is sometimes referred to as PESTEL. The additional 'E' is for environmental factors (included as part of social factors in PEST) and the additional 'L' is for the legal factors (included as part of the political factors in PEST).

(b) Porter's five forces

Approach to industry level analysis.

Stakeholders

Stakeholders are anyone affected by the organisation and its activities.

Managing stakeholders – Mendelow's matrix

The interest and power of different stakeholder groups can affect an organisation's performance.

Consideration of stakeholders is important:

- The **mission and objectives** of the organisation need to be developed with the needs of stakeholders in mind.

- The requirements, power and ambitions of stakeholders will **influence the organisation's ability to implement strategy**.

- Managers must deal with the **conflict** through:

  - **prioritisation** – this could follow from Mendelow's matrix

  - **negotiation and 'satisficing'** – finding the minimum acceptable outcome for each group to achieve a compromise

  - **sequential attention** – each period a different stakeholder group is focused upon

  - **side payments** – this can often involve benefiting a group without giving them what they actually want

  - exercise of power.

- The management of stakeholders will have a **direct impact on objectives and key performance indicators (KPIs)**.

- The interests of different stakeholder groups might **affect the areas of performance that are measured**.

Ethical Issues

ETHICS

Ethical behaviour reduces risk
and the organisation is likely
to be favoured by existing and
potential customers, employees,
business partners and investors.

**CORPORATE SOCIAL
RESPONSIBILITY (CSR)**

CSR is giving the stakeholders
more than the legal minimum,
e.g. donating funds to charity
and becoming carbon neutral.
Benefits are customer goodwill,
better reputation, happy
employees and less chance of
legislation being passed.

The impact of government policy

Government policy is a key ingredient in the political environment facing enterprises.

- Taxation levels.
- Interest rates.
- Exchange rates.
- Incentive schemes.
- Public expenditure levels.
- Environment protection.
- Restrictive practices.
- Consumer and worker protection.

The impact of fiscal and monetary policy

MACROECONOMIC POLICY

- The management of the economy by the government.
- Aims are full employment, price stability, economic growth and appropriate distribution of income and wealth.
- Influences level of aggregate demand using:

MONETARY POLICY

The government adjusts the money supply, interest rates, exchange rates & availability of credit.

FISCAL POLICY

The government adjusts taxation, public spending and public borrowing.

The impact of government regulation

Government regulation includes: • competition policy • supply-side policies • green policies.

Competition policy
Government's response to actual or potential monopoly power

Public provision of services: e.g. nationalisation of a number of UK banks in 2008/9

Self-regulation: e.g. legal and accountancy professions

Public regulation, especially of privatised services:
- Setting a limit on price increases
- Agreeing investment targets
- Framework of KPIs with rewards and penalties

The control of monopolies: e.g. the UK Competition Act prohibits anti-competitive agreements (such as illegal cartels) and prohibits the abuse of a dominant position

Supply-side policies

- Largely anti-regulation and anti-government interference.
- Based on the view that regulation prevents the efficient and effective working of the economy.

Green policies

- Growing area of government intervention.
- Response to external environmental costs of production and consumption, i.e. negative externalities.
- Examples are carbon taxes, emission targets and penalties.

Risk and uncertainty

Risk is the variability of possible returns. There are a number of possible outcomes and the probability of each outcome is known. All businesses face risk/uncertainty. Risk management is the process of understanding and managing the risks that an organisation is inevitably subject to.

Uncertainty also means there are a number of possible outcomes. However, the probability of each outcome is not known.

Exogenous variables are variables that do not originate from within the organisation itself and are not controllable by management, e.g. government policy, social factors.

Scenario planning

– looks at a number of different but plausible future situations.

Maximin – involves selecting the alternative that maximises the minimum pay-off achievable. Useful for risk averse decision makers.

Maximax – involves selecting the alternative that maximises the maximum pay-off achievable. Useful for risk seekers.

Minimax regret – is the strategy that minimises the maximum regret.

Dealing with risk/uncertainty

Computer simulations

– a modelling technique which shows the effect of more than one variable changing at a time and gives management a view of the likely range of outcomes.

Sensitivity analysis

– takes each uncertain factor in turn, and calculates the change that would be necessary in that factor before the original decision is reversed.

Expected values (EVs)

– shows the weighted average of all possible outcomes

$EV = \Sigma px$

x = outcome

p = probability of outcome

Useful for a risk-neutral decision maker

Shareholders will generally be risk seeking.

Banks are generally risk averse and will want security over their funds.

Impact of risk appetite of stakeholders on performance management

Employees and managers may be risk averse (if, say, job security is important) or risk seeking (if, say, there is a promise of a huge bonus.

Venture capitalists are rational investors who want maximum return for minimal risk but they will be prepared for some investments to fail.

Exam focus

Exam sitting	Area examined	Question number	Number of marks
June 2015	Expected values, uncertainty	1(iii), (iv)	16
December 2014	Stakeholders	1(ii)	14
June 2014	Risk	3(a)(b)	17
December 2013	PEST	1(ii)	11
June 2013	Porter's 5 forces and risk	3(a)(c)	21
December 2011	Risk	1	35
June 2011	Stakeholders	2(c)	6
December 2010	PEST	4(a)	4
June 2010	Expected values	2(b)(i)(ii)	12
December 2009	Economic, financial and social considerations	4(b)	14
June 2009	Maximax, maximin and minimax regret	2(d)	7
December 2008	Ethical issues/CSR, how government can aid business performance	3(c)(d)	10

June 2008	Strategic and economic factors	3(a)	14
December 2007	Porter's 5 forces	5(a)	10
Pilot paper	Ethics	1(d)	3
Pilot	Ethics	1(d)	3
Pilot paper	Risk	3(b)	10

3

Approaches to budgets

In this chapter

- Purposes of budgeting.
- Participation in budgeting setting.
- Budgeting methods.

This section of the paper draws on technical knowledge from previous papers on different approaches to budgeting, but the emphasis of P5 is on the practical issues relating to the choice of an appropriate method, the impact of budgeting approaches on behaviour and whether organisations should move 'beyond budgeting'.

Questions may be asked on particular methods of budgeting such as zero-based or activity-based budgets.

Purposes of budgeting

A **budget** is a quantitative plan prepared for a specific time period.

Budgeting serves a number of purposes:

- Planning
- Control
- Communication
- Co-ordination
- Evaluation
- Motivation
- Authorisation
- Delegation

Participation in budget setting

A **top-down** budget is one that is imposed on the budget holder by senior management.

Advantages:

- Avoids budgetary slack
- Avoids dysfunctional behaviour
- Senior Managers retain control
- Can be quicker
- Avoids problem of bad decisions by inexperienced managers

A **bottom-up** budget involves divisonal managers participating in the setting of the budgets.

Advantages:

- Improved motivation
- Increases divisional manager's understanding
- Frees up senior management resources
- Uses local knowledge

Budgeting Methods

Fixed – when a budget is prepared for a single level of activity.

Flexible – budget prepared with the cost behaviour of all elements known and classified as either fixed or variable. The budget may be flexed to the actual level of activity.

Rolling – kept continually up to date by adding another period when the earliest period has expired.

Incremental – starts with previous period's budget or actual results and adds or subtracts an incremental amount.

Activity-based budgeting (ABB)

Definition

ABB uses the principles of ABC to estimate the firm's future demand for resources and hence can help the firm to acquire these resources more efficiently.

Steps involved:

1   Estimate the production and sales volumes of individual products or customers.

2   Estimate the demand for organisational activities.

3   Determine the resources that are required to perform organisational activities.

4   Estimate for each resource the quantity that must be supplied to meet demand.

5   Take action to adjust the capacity of resources to match projected supply.

Advantages	Disadvantages
• Draws attention to the costs of 'overhead activities'.	• May require considerable time and effort.
• It provides information for the control of activity costs, by assuming that they are variable, (long-term).	• May not be appropriate for all organisations.
• Emphasises that activity costs may be controllable if volume is controlled.	• May be difficult to assign responsibilities for activities to individual budget holders.
• Can be useful for TQM since it relates the cost of an activity to the level of service provided.	• In the short-term many overhead costs are not variable.

Zero-based budgeting

Definition

Zero-based budgeting (ZBB) is a method of budgeting that requires each cost element to be specifically justified, as though the activities to which the budget relates were being undertaken for the first time. Without approval, the budget allowance is zero.

The steps

1   Managers specify for their responsibility centres those activities that can be individually evaluated.

2   Describe each of the individual activities in a decision package which should:

   •   state the costs and benefits expected

   •   be drawn up in such a way that it can be evaluated and ranked

3   Evaluate and rank each decision package, usually using cost/benefit analysis

4   Allocate resources to the various packages.

Advantages	Disadvantages
• Inefficient or obsolete operations can be identified and discontinued.	• Time & cost involved.
• ZBB leads to increased staff involvement at all levels, improving motivation and communication.	• Emphasis on short-term benefits to the detriment of long-term benefits.
• It responds to a change in the business environment.	• Management skills needed.
• Knowledge and understanding of cost-behaviour improved.	• Rankings of packages may be subjective where the benefits are of a qualitative nature.
• Resources should be allocated economically and efficiently.	• Difficult to compare and rank completely different types of activity.
	• The budgeting process may become too rigid.
	• Managers may feel demotivated due to the large amount of time spent on the budgeting process.

Public sector budgeting

Approaches used

- Incremental budgeting is traditional approach.
- ZBB and planned programme budgeting (where work is broken down into programmes designed to achieve certain objectives).

Exam sitting	Area examined	Question number	Number of marks
Sept/Dec 2015	Weaknesses in budgeting system	2(a)	13
Jun 2013	ABC and ABM	2	25
Dec 2012	Budgeting	2	25
Jun 2010	ABC and ABM	4	20
Jun 2010	Calculation of budgeted net profit/(loss)	2(a)	7
Dec 2009	Preparation of actual and budgeted income statement	1(i)	10
Dec 2008	ABC and ABM	5	20
Jun 2008	Problems with budgeting	2	24
Dec 2007	Forecasting	3(a)	5
Dec 2007	ABC	4(b)(c)	15
Pilot	Actual vs budget comparison	1(a)	14

Business structure and performance management

In this chapter

- Performance management in different business structures.
- The needs of modern service industries.
- Business integration.
- Business process re-engineering.

You need to be able to assess and discuss the relationship between business structure and management accounting requirements.

Performance management in different business structures

	Functional organisations	Divisional organisations
Information needs	• Centralised. • Performance information required by top of organisation for planning and control. • Data aggregated at the highest level before feedback given.	• Decentralised. • Greater participation lower down the organisation. • Information needs to be available lower down organisation.
Advantages for performance management	• Easier to assess and control performance of functions.	• Easier to assess divisional/SBU performance. • Performance management can be tailored to local needs.
Problems for performance management	• Difficult to assess performance of individual products or markets. • Unsuitable for diversified organisations.	• Transfer pricing issues. • Issue of allocation of central costs. • Potential problems with lack of goal congruence.

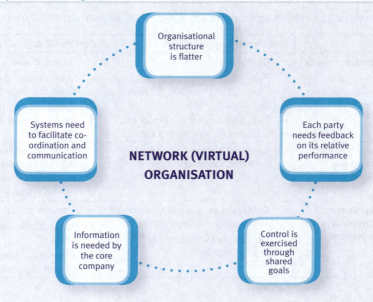

The influence of organisational structure on information requirements

Organisational characteristics	Impact on performance management system
Large, complex	Sophisticated performance management systems
High level of interaction between business units	Performance management system needs to: • support communication between units • provide common language.
Autonomous business units	Systems adapted to individual approach

Problems associated with complex business structures

Business structure	Problems
Joint venture	• Different partners may have different goals so a variety of performance measures will be required. • Attributing accountability is difficult. • Reporting of profits/ losses difficult if partners won't share information. • Quality, cost control and risk management difficult if partners have different opinions. • Security of information a concern.

Strategic alliance	• Independence retained making it difficult to put common performance measures in place. • Security of confidential information.
Multinationals	• Open to greater levels of uncertainty, e.g. due to exchange rate movements.

The needs of modern service industries

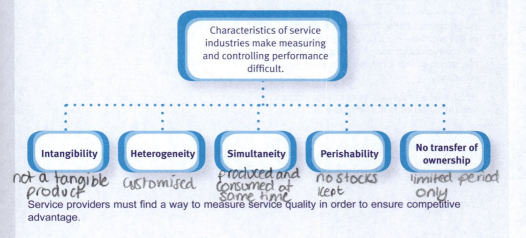

Characteristics of service industries make measuring and controlling performance difficult.

Intangibility	Heterogeneity	Simultaneity	Perishability	No transfer of ownership
not a tangible product	customised	produced and consumed at same time	no stocks kept	limited period only

Service providers must find a way to measure service quality in order to ensure competitive advantage.

Business integration

Definition

Business integration means that all aspects of the business must be aligned to secure the most efficient use of the organisation's resources so that it can achieve its objectives effectively.

Processes are viewed as complete entities from initial order to final delivery.

Porter's value chain

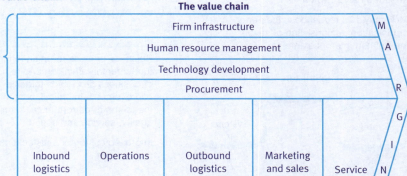

The value chain

Firm infrastructure					M
Human resource management					A
Technology development					
Procurement					R
					G
					I
Inbound logistics	Operations	Outbound logistics	Marketing and sales	Service	N

Primary activities

The value chain model

- Shows how each activity adds to competitive advantage.
- Emphasises linkages and critical success factors within activities and for the value chain as a whole.
- Can be used for ongoing performance management as targets can be set and monitored for different activities.

Mckinsey's 7s model

Mckinsey's 7s model describes an organisation as consisting of seven interrelated internal elements.

How the company is organised

Structure
HARD

what the company does

Strategy
HARD

procedures

Systems
HARD

Culture

Shared values
SOFT

what skills are needed

Skills
SOFT

Management style

Style
SOFT

what staff?

Staff
SOFT

Business process re-engineering (BPR)

Definition

Business process re-engineering is the fundamental rethinking and radical redesign of business processes to achieve dramatic improvements in critical, contemporary measures of performance, such as cost, quality, service and speed.

Improved customer satisfaction is often the primary aim.

The influence of BPR on the organisation:

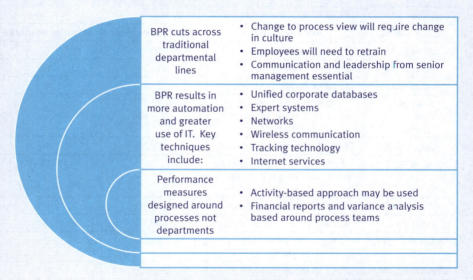

BPR cuts across traditional departmental lines	• Change to process view will require change in culture • Employees will need to retrain • Communication and leadership from senior management essential
BPR results in more automation and greater use of IT. Key techniques include:	• Unified corporate databases • Expert systems • Networks • Wireless communication • Tracking technology • Internet services
Performance measures designed around processes not departments	• Activity-based approach may be used • Financial reports and variance analysis based around process teams

Exam sitting	Area examined	Question number	Number of marks
June 2015	Value chain	1(v)	6
June 2014	BPR	2(a)(b)	17
June 2014	Complex business structures	3(c)	8
June 2013	Differences between services and manufacturing organisations	1(i)	5
June 2013	Change in divisional structure	4(c)	9
June 2012	Performance management and measurement in complex business structures	5	17
June 2012	Complex business structures	5	17
June 2010	Characteristics of services	3(iii)	8
December 2009	Measurement of service quality	5(c)	3
December 2008	Service quality	2(c)(d)	10

5

The impact of information technology

In this chapter

- Sources of management information.
- Compatibility of management accounting and management accounting information.
- Developing management accounting systems.
- The need for continual systems development.
- Recent IT developments.
- Instant access to data.
- Remote input of data.

Sources of management information

Information can be obtained from internal and external sources. Much is free, but some comes at a cost, such as:

- most information from business enquiry agents is charged for
- banks and financial journals often sell surveys and forecasts
- internet databases may charge a subscription
- government statistics, forecasts and reports may be charged for.

Internal sources	External sources
• Sales ledger system	• Suppliers
• Purchase ledger system	• Newspapers and journals
• Payroll system	• Government
• Fixed asset system	• Customers
• Production	• Employees
• Sales and marketing	• Banks
	• Business enquiry agents
	• Internet

Compatibility of management accounting and management accounting information

Management accounting information may be used to:

- assess performance
- value inventories
- make future plans
- control the business
- make decisions.

Management accounting involves the provision and analysis of detailed information to help managers to run the business today and in the future.

The objectives of management accounting should be compatible with management accounting information.

Developing management accounting systems

Definition

A management information system (MIS) converts internal and external data into useful information which is then communicated to managers at all levels and across all functions to enable them to make timely and effective decisions for planning, directing and controlling activities.

There are a number of types of MIS:

Executive information system (EIS)

- Gives senior managers access to internal and external information
- Presented in a user-friendly summarised form
- Option to drill down to a greater level of detail

Decision support system (DSS)

- Aids managers in making decisions
- Predicts the consequences of a number of possible scenarios
- Manager then uses their judgement to make the final decision

Expert system

- Hold specialist knowledge
- Allow non-experts to interrogate for information, advice and recommended decisions

The need for continual systems development

Information and accounting systems need to be developed continually otherwise they will become out of date.

Recent IT developments

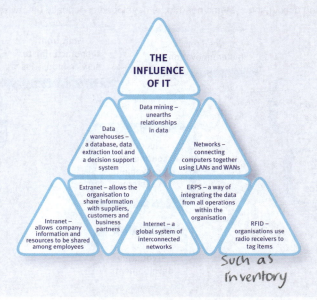

THE INFLUENCE OF IT

Data mining – unearths relationships in data

Data warehouses – a database, data extraction tool and a decision support system

Networks – connecting computers together using LANs and WANs

Extranet – allows the organisation to share information with suppliers, customers and business partners

ERPS – a way of integrating the data from all operations within the organisation

Intranet – allows company information and resources to be shared among employees

Internet – a global system of interconnected networks

RFID – organisations use radio receivers to tag items

Such as inventory

Instant access to data

The information systems discussed provide
instant access to previously unavailable
data that can be used for benchmarking and
control purposes.

The budgetary control system

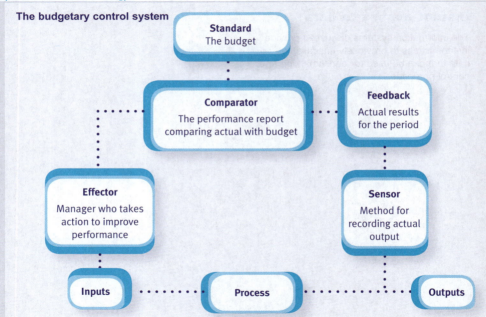

Standard
The budget

Comparator
The performance report comparing actual with budget

Feedback
Actual results for the period

Effector
Manager who takes action to improve performance

Sensor
Method for recording actual output

Inputs

Process

Outputs

Remote input of data

New data capture techniques allow non-finance specialists to remotely input management accounting data into an organisation's system. For example:

- Mobile sales staff can record orders using laptops or hand held computers.

- Shop floor sales staff use multi-purpose barcode scanners to collect information about what products are being bought, at what time and by which customers.

Exam sitting	Area examined	Question number	Number of marks
June 2015	ERPS	2(a)	10
December 2013	RFID	3(a)	12
December 2011	Control and development of IS	3	20
June 2011	EIS	1(c)	5
December 2010	Impact of KPIs on system design	1(d)	9
June 2010	IT systems and ABC	4(a)(ii)	4

chapter

6

Performance reports for management

In this chapter

- Reports for performance management.
- Dealing with qualitative data.
- Problems of performance measurement.

The output reports (performance reports) produced from a management information system need to be tailored to suit the needs of the users of those reports.

Qualitative information is an important component of a performance report but is often ignored due to its highly subjective nature.

The undesirable behavioural consequences of a poorly designed performance measurement system also need to be considered.

Reports for performance management

The information must match the purpose. A range of financial and non-financial (quantitative and qualitative) information should be included.

The audience should be considered – the report should be relevant and understandable for the audience.

Considerations when designing a performance report:

The layout should be user friendly and avoid information overload.

The purpose of the report should be considered – does it reflect the mission and objectives?

Dealing with qualitative data

Definition

Qualitative information is information that cannot normally be expressed in numerical terms.

Qualitative information is often in the form of opinions, e.g. from:

- customers
- employees
- suppliers.

The **subjective** nature of qualitative information makes it more difficult to consider.

Although difficult, qualitative factors should be considered when making a decision.

KAPLAN PUBLISHING

Problems of performance measurement

Performance measurement systems can distort the processes they are meant to serve. A poorly-designed system can lead to dysfunctional behaviour.

Sending wrong signals can result in inappropriate action.

- Misrepresentation. – creative reporting 90% of users.. only small sample
- Gaming. – trying to meet individual targets
- Misinterpretation. – failure to recognise some factors eg) non financial
- Short-termism (mypoia).
- Measure fixation.
- Tunnel vision. focus only on measures
- Sub-optimisation. focus on some measures so others fail
- Ossification (lack of flexibility). reluctant to change

A number of actions can be taken to minimise the impact of these imperfections or to avoid them in the first place.

Exam focus

Exam sitting	Area examined	Question number	Number of marks
June 2015	Reward systems	3(c)	9
December 2014	Qualitative factors	2(c)	7
June 2014	Evaluation of performance report	1(i)	15
December 2013	Wrong signals and dysfunctional behaviour	2(b)	10
June 2013	Evaluation of strategic performance report	1(ii)	8
June 2012	Assessment of performance report	1(i)	12
December 2011	Suitability of branch information given	4(a)	8

7

Human resources aspects of performance management

In this chapter

- Human resources management (HRM).
- Using appraisal to improve business performance.
- Reward scheme for employees and managers.
- Management styles.

This chapter looks at the link between HRM and performance management and considers the impact of the appraisal system and the reward system on the behaviour of employees and on the organisation. It also discusses the need to consider management style when designing a system.

Human resource management (HRM)

HRM is the strategic and coherent approach to the management of an organisation's most valued assets: the people working there who individually and collectively contribute to the achievement of its objectives for sustainable competitive advantage.

Recruitment involves attracting a field of suitable candidates for the job where as selection is aimed at choosing the best person for the job from the field of candidates sourced at recruitment.

A **competency framework** shows a set of behaviour patterns and skills that the candidate needs in order to perform a job with competence.

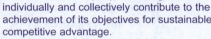

Today, employees are seen less as an expensive necessity but as a strategic resource that might provide the organisation with competitive advantage.

People are fundamental to an organisation

Strategic significance
- the creation and fulfilment of the strategy relies on the skills, knowledge and creativity of the people.

Operational significance
- successful completion of a task relies on having employees with appropriate skills and abilities to carry out their work.

Using appraisal to improve business perfomance

Reasons for appraisals

Control
- Strategic objectives of organisations are linked to goals of employees.

Identify development needs
- Appraisal identifies employees' training and development needs.

The following are difficulties in appraisals.

Appraisal is:
- Confrontation
- Judgement
- Chat
- Bureaucracy
- An event
- Unfinished business

Steps should be taken to address these issues.

Three approaches to measuring employee performance:

- Measurement of inputs
- Behaviour in performance
- Measurements of results and outcomes

Motivated staff are more likely to achieve targets and organisational goals

$$\underset{\text{(strength motivation)}}{\text{Force}} = \underset{\text{(individual's desire for outcome)}}{\text{Valence}} \times \underset{\substack{\text{(probability will achieve}\\\text{outcomes)}}}{\text{Expectance}}$$

KAPLAN PUBLISHIN

Rewards scheme for employees and managers

Help organisation achieve strategy/ objectives

To comply with law and ethical obligations

Help recruitment/ retention

Aims of a reward system

Fair and consistent

Control salary costs

To motivate staff

To reward performance

Methods:

- Basic pay
- Performance – related pay (PRP):
  - Piecework
  - Individual PRP
  - Group PRP
- Knowledge contingent pay
- Commission
- Profit-related pay
- Benefits
- Share options

Linking reward schemes to performance:

Benefits	Problems
<ul><li>Motivates staff</li><li>Attracts staff</li><li>Makes it clear what creates organisational success</li><li>Focus on continuous improvement</li></ul>	<ul><li>Employees prioritise achievement of reward</li><li>Unmotivated if target outside of employee control</li><li>Potential stress</li><li>Potential dysfunctional behaviour</li><li>How to set targets</li></ul>

Rewards should be aligned with strategic goals. Changes in the modern business environment include a focus on:

- Quality
- Process re-design
- E-business

Management styles

Hopwood identified three distinct management styles of performance appraisal. The style needs to be considered when designing an effective performance management system.

- Budget constrained – short-term financial performance is measured using, say, ROCE.
- Profit-conscious – measures of long-term profitability, such as NPV, may be used.
- Non-accounting – non-financial measures, such as customer satisfaction, are used.

Exam sitting	Area examined	Question number	Number of marks
June 2014	Appraisals	2(c)	8
December 2012	Reward schemes	1(iii)	10
December 2011	Performance appraisal system, Hopwood	4(b)(c)	12
December 2009	Acceptance of a performance measurement system	1(iii)	6
June 2009	Agency and expectancy theory	3(a)	12

8

Financial performance measures in the private sector

In this chapter

- Objectives of a profit-seeking organisation.
- Financial measures of performance.
- Liquidity and gearing.
- Short- and long-term financial performance.

In the exam, you may be required to look at performance measures from a variety of contexts. In this chapter we focus on the principle financial measures used by the private sector.

Objectives of a profit-seeking organisation

Main objective of a business is to maximise shareholder wealth.

- Shareholders are the legal owners of the company.

- They are concerned with the following aspects of financial performance:

    – current earnings

    – future earnings

    – dividend policy

    – relative risk of the investment.

Wealth maximisation can be translated into three sub-objectives

Profit
Often short-term focus

Growth and development
Which results in improved financial performance

Survival
Long-term goal – continuing in existence

Financial measures of performance

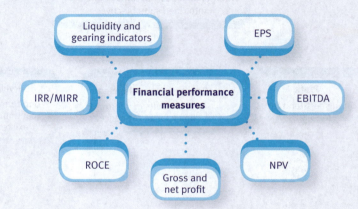

Indicator	Advantages	Disadvantages
ROCE – Return on capital employed ROCE = $\dfrac{\text{Profit from operations}}{\text{Capital employed}} \times 100$ Use PBIT if net profit is not given. Capital employed = total assets less current liabilities or total equity plus long-term debt.	• Simple to calculate. • Figures are readily available. • Measure how well a business is using the funds invested in it. • Often used by external analysts/investors.	• Poor correlation between ROCE and shareholder value. • Care must be taken to ensure that like is compared with like e.g. inclusion of intangibles in capital employed. • Can be distorted by accounting policies. • Can be improved by cutting back investment – may lead to short-termism.
Earnings per share (EPS) EPS = $\dfrac{\text{PAT – preference dividends}}{\text{weighted ave. number of ordinary shares in issue}}$	• Easily understood by shareholders. • Calculation is precisely defined by accounting standards.	• Accounting treatment may cause ratios to be distorted.

	• Figures are readily available. • Widely used.	• Poor correlation between EPS growth and shareholder value.
EBITDA Earnings before interest, tax and depreciation adjustment.	• Measures underlying performance. • Ignores impact of tax, interest and depreciation. • Easy to calculate. • Easy to understand.	• Ignores changes in working capital. • Fails to consider the amount of fixed asset replacement needed by the business. • Can easily be manipulated.
NPV • Based on DCF analysis.	• Strong correlation with shareholder value. • It considers the time value of money.	• Difficult to calculate/ understand.

• Looks at present value of cash inflows less present value of outflows of project. • Any project with a positive NPV is viable.	• Risk can be considered. • Cash flows less subject to manipulation and subjective decisions than accounting profits. • Considers all cash flows of a project. • Superior measure to IRR.	• It does not easily allow two projects of very different scales to be compared. • It is based on assumptions about cash flow, the timing and the cost of capital. • Challenging to use for target-setting.
IRR • Discount rate when NPV = 0. • Accept project if IRR > firm's cost of capital.	• Provides alternative to NPV when cost of capital of project is uncertain. $IRR = L + \dfrac{NPVL}{NPVL - NPVH} \times (H - L)$	• Possible to get multiple rates of return.
MIRR • Represents the actual return generated by a project.	• Eliminates the problems associated with IRR.	

$$MIRR = (Pv \text{ of inflows} \div Pv \text{ of outflows})^{\frac{1}{n}} \times (1 + \text{cost of capital}) - 1$$

(n = project life in years)

Other profitability ratios

Used alongside main measures such as ROCE.

Asset turnover	$\dfrac{\text{Sales}}{\text{Capital employed}}$
Dividend cover	$\dfrac{\text{PAT}}{\text{Dividends paid during the year}}$
Dividend yield	$\dfrac{\text{Dividend per share}}{\text{Current share price}} \times 100\%$
P/E ratio	$\dfrac{\text{Share price}}{\text{EPS}}$
Earnings yield	$\dfrac{\text{EPS}}{\text{Share price}} \times 100\%$
Return on equity	$\dfrac{\text{Net profit after tax}}{\text{Average shareholder's equity}}$

Liquidity and gearing

Liquidity

There is often a trade-off between liquidity and profitability. Liquidity needs to be considered alongside profitability when assessing a company's financial situation.

Current ratio	$\dfrac{\text{Current assets}}{\text{Current liabilities}}$
Acid test (quick ratio)	$\dfrac{\text{Current assets} - \text{inventories}}{\text{Current liabilities}}$
Raw material period	$\dfrac{\text{Average value of raw materials}}{\text{Purchases}} \times 365$
WIP period	$\dfrac{\text{Average value of WIP}}{\text{Cost of sales}} \times 365$
Finished goods period	$\dfrac{\text{Average value of finished}}{\text{Cost of sales}} \times 365$

Receivables period	$\dfrac{\text{Average receivables}}{\text{Sales revenue}} \times 365$
Payables period	$\dfrac{\text{Average payables}}{\text{Purchases}} \times 365$

Risk ratios

These ratios measure the ability of the company to meet its long-term liabilities

Financial gearing	$\dfrac{\text{Long-term debt (LTD)}}{\text{Shareholders' funds}} \times 100\%$ or $\dfrac{\text{LTD}}{\text{LTD + Shareholders' funds}} \times 100\%$
Operating gearing	$\dfrac{\text{Fixed costs}}{\text{Variable costs}}$
Interest cover	$\dfrac{\text{PBIT}}{\text{Interest charges}}$

KAPLAN PUBLISHING

Short- and long-term financial performance

WAYS TO REDUCE SHORT – TERMISM.

Incorporate both financial and non-financial measures, for example via a balanced scorecard approach.

Switch from a budget – constrained to a profit – conscious or non-accounting style (Hopwood).

Give managers share options to focus their attention on longer-term factors.

Link bonuses to profits over longer timescales than one year.

Ensure that potential investments are assessed on the basis of NPV.

Reduce the degree of decentralisation to ensure stronger central control.

Incorporate value-based management techniques.

Exam sitting	Area examined	Question number	Number of marks
Jun 2014	Fixed and variable costs	1(ii)	6
Jun 2013	Evaluation of strategic performance report and metrics	1(ii)	8
Dec 2012	ROCE	3(b)	7
Dec 2012	Financial performance evaluation and choice of measures	1(i)(ii)	20
Jun 2012	Evaluation of performance measures	1(ii)(iii)	24
Dec 2009	Evaluation of financial performance	4(a)	6
Jun 2009	NPV calculation	2(a)	6
Dec 2008	Assessment of financial performance	2(a)	14
Jun 2008	NPV and sensitivity analysis	4(i)(ii)	8
Pilot paper	Assessment of financial performance and EBITDA	4	20

chapter

9

Divisional performance appraisal and transfer pricing

In this chapter

- Problems associated with divisional structures.
- Responsibility accounting.
- Divisional performance measures.
- Value-based management.
- Transfer pricing.

Many modern businesses are split into divisions. You need to be able to discuss the problems that may arise as a result of a divisional structure, the methods that can be used to appraise performance and the use of a value based management approach.

You need to be able to discuss the advantages and disadvantages of transfer pricing systems, the behavioural issues associated with them, and how to design a system. This may require you to generate a simple transfer pricing example to illustrate the issues.

Problems associated with divisional structures

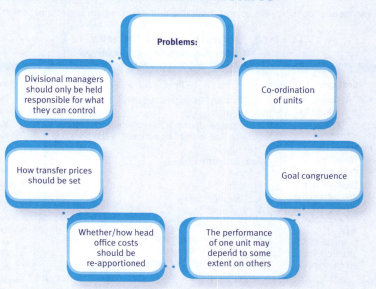

Problems:

- Co-ordination of units
- Goal congruence
- The performance of one unit may depend to some extent on others
- Whether/how head office costs should be re-apportioned
- How transfer prices should be set
- Divisional managers should only be held responsible for what they can control

Responsibility accounting

A manager should only be held accountable and assessed on aspects of performance they control.

Types of responsibility centre

Cost centre

- Division incurs costs but has no revenue stream.

Measures:
- Total cost
- Cost variances
- Cost per unit and other cost ratios, NFPIs, for example, related to quality, productivity, efficiency.

Profit centre

- Division has both costs and revenue.
- Manager does not have the authority to alter the level of investment in the division.

Measures:
As cost centre PLUS
- Sales
- Profit
- Sales variances
- Margins
- Market share
- Working capital ratios (depending on the division concerned)
- NFPIs related to customer satisfaction.

Investment centre

- Division has both costs and revenue.
- Manager does have the authority to invest in new assets or dispose of existing ones.

Measures:
As profit centre PLUS
- Return on investment (ROI)
- Residual income (RI)
- Economic value added (EVA).

Divisional performance measures

Measure	Advantages	Disadvantages
Return on investment (ROI) (Controllable profit from operations/ controllable capital employed) × 100% Decision: accept project if ROI > cost of capital	• Widely used and accepted. • Enables comparisons. • Can be broken down into secondary ratios.	• May lead to dysfunctional decision making. • Depreciation methods will result in ROI improving with the age of an asset (use annuity depreciation). • Different accounting policies can confuse comparisons. • Excludes intangible assets from capital employed. • Corporate objectives of maximising shareholders' wealth are not achieved by making decisions on the basis of ROI. • May encourage the manipulation of profit and capital employed.

Measure	Advantages	Disadvantages
Residual income (RI) Controllable profit from operations X less: imputed interest X RI X • Imputed interest = controllable capital employed × cost of capital. • Decision: accept the project, if the RI is positive.	• Reduces the problems of ROI, i.e. dysfunctional behaviour and holding on to old assets. • Highlights cost of financing a division. • Different cost of capitals can be applied to different divisions based on their risk profiles.	• Does not take into account the size of the investment or organisation. • Different accounting policies can confuse comparisons. • It is difficult to decide upon an appropriate cost of capital. • May encourage manipulation of profit and capital employed. • It does not always result in decisions that are in the best interests of the company.

Measure	Advantages	Disadvantages
Economic value added (EVA) NOPAT X Adjusted value of capital employed at start of year × WACC (X) EVA X • A similar but superior measure to RI. • Decision: accept the project if the EVA is positive.	• The adjustments made avoid distortion by accounting policies and should therefore result in goal congruent decisions. • Emphasises cost of financing to division's manager. • EVA is consistant with NPV and should create real wealth for shareholders. • Long-term value-adding expenditure can be capitalised, removing any incentive for managers to take a short-term view.	• Many assumptions made when calculating WACC. • Requires numerous adjustments to profit and capital employed figures. • Absolute measure (as is RI) so divisional comparisons difficult. • Based on historical data where as shareholders are interested in future performance.

How to calculate EVA

NOPAT

Controllable operating profit	X
Add:	
accounting depreciation	X
increase in provisions	X
non-cash expenses	X
advertising, r&d, employee training	X
operating lease payments	X
Deduct:	
economic depreciation	(X)
decrease in provisions	(X)
amortisation of advertising, r&d and employee training	(X)
depreciation of operating lease payments	(X)
tax paid including lost tax relief on interest	(X)
= NOPAT	X

Adjusted value of capital employed at the beginning of the year

Main adjustments to capital employed figure are:

- adjustment to reflect replacement cost of non-current assets rather than the book value

- adjustment to reflect economic and not accounting depreciation

- add back value of provisions in period

- add non-cash expenses to retained profit at the end of the year

- increase for expenditure on advertising, r&d and employee training

- add present value of future lease payments.

WACC

- WACC = (proportion of equity x cost of equity) + (proportion of debt x post tax cost of debt).

Value-based management

Definition

Value-based management (VBM) is an approach to management whereby the company's strategy, objectives and processes are aligned to help the company focus on **key drivers** of shareholder wealth and hence maximise this value.

Measure shareholder value using:

- Economic value added (EVA)
- Market value added (MVA)
- Shareholder value analysis

Techniques for increasing and monitoring value include:

- The balanced scorecard
- Business process re-engineering
- ABC and ABM
- TQM
- JIT
- Benchmarking

Implementing VBM:

- Develop a strategy to maximise value
- Value drivers indentified and long-term and short-term performance targets are defined for these drivers
- A plan is developed to achieve these targets
- Performance metrics and reward systems are created compatible with these targets.

Transfer pricing

Transfer price

- The price at which goods and services are transferred from one division to another in the same organisation.

Characteristics of a good transfer price:

- Goal congruence

- Fair for divisions

- Autonomy for divisions

- Assists book keeping

- Minimises global tax liability

General rules for setting transfer prices

Perfect competition in market for intermediate product

- Transfer at market price.

Surplus capacity

- Minimum price selling division will accept = marginal cost.
- Maximum price the buying division will pay is the lower of the external purchase price (if available) and the net marginal revenue.

Production constraints

- Minimum price selling division will accept = marginal cost + lost contribution from other product.
- Maximum price the buying division will pay is the lower of the external purchase price (if available) and the net marginal revenue.

Practical methods of transfer pricing

Cost plus

- Producer calculates unit cost.
- May add margin to guarantee profit.
- Use standard cost to avoid passing on inefficiencies and ensure variances reported in division responsible.

Market price based

- Perfect competition for product.
- Division's product must be same as offered by market.
- Adjust market price for costs not incurred on internal transfer.

Issue

- Selling division wants to use total cost to ensure recover fixed overheads.
- Buying division will not want to be charged for fixed costs.

Solutions

- Two part tariff – the selling division transfers each unit at marginal cost and a periodic transfer is made to cover fixed costs.
- Dual pricing – selling and buying divisions record different transfer prices.

International transfer pricing

Important because almost 2/3 world trade takes place within multi-national companies. Issues are:

- taxation
- remittance controls.

Taxation

- Altering the transfer price between divisions in different countries moves profit between countries.
- Anti-avoidance legislation tax authorities can treat the transaction as having taken place at a fair 'arms length' price and revise the profits accordingly.

Remittance controls

- Government of host country in which investment has been made imposes restriction on amount of profit returned to the parent company. This limits parent's ability to pay dividends to shareholders.

- May be done through exchange controls.
- May be avoided by:
  - increasing transfer prices paid by foreign subsidiary
  - lending equivalent of dividend to parent company
  - making payments to parent in other forms, for example management charges.
- Foreign government may try to prevent the above measures.

Exam focus

Exam sitting	Area examined	Question number	Number of marks
Sept/Dec 2015	EVA	1(i)	15
June 2015	EVA, ROI and RI	4	25
June 2014	EVA and VBM	1(iii)(iv)	19
June 2013	Transfer pricing	4	25
December 2012	EVA	3(a)	13
June 2012	EVA	1(ii)	3
June 2011	RI, ROI, EVA, transfer pricing	1(a)(b)	24
December 2010	EVA and VBM	3	20
December 2009	Transfer pricing	3	20
December 2008	Transfer pricing	4(a)	12
June 2008	ROI, RI and EVA	1(a)(i)(ii)	20
December 2007	Divisional performance measures, RI and EVA	2	25

KAPLAN PUBLISHING

10

Performance management in not-for-profit organisations

In this chapter

- What is a not-for-profit organisation?
- Problems associated with performance measurement.
- The use of league tables (benchmarking) in the public sector.

Exam focus

You need to be able to discuss the issues which affect not-for-profit organisations and the implications of these for performance management.

What is a not-for-profit organisation?

Profit is not the main objective.

Performance considers both financial and non-financial issues.

Most do not have external shareholders.

NOT FOR PROFIT

Public sector e.g. healthcare, defence, education, museums.

They do not distribute dividends.

Private sector e.g. charities and sports associations.

Objectives include some social, cultural, philanthropic, welfare or environmental dimension.

Problems associated with performance measurement

1. Many of the benefits and costs are non- quantifiable. Many orgaisations use cost benefit analysis to quantify these items in financial terms.

4. Impact of politics on performance measurement
- organisations suffer political interference
- long-term objectives sacrificed for short-term political gain.

FOUR KEY PROBLEMS

2. Assessing value for money, especially in public sector organisations receiving a fixed budget for spending from government.

3. Objectives are:
- diverse i.e. different organisations will have different objectives
- multiple – need prioritise and compromise between the different needs of multiple stakeholders.

KAPLAN PUBLISHING

Assessing value for money (VFM).

Definition

VFM measures whether the organisation has met stakeholders' expectation of best value for the limited funds available.

Assessing value for money can be achieved by:

- analysing economy, efficiency and effectiveness (the 3Es)
- benchmarking
- using performance indicators
- conducting VFM studies
- comparing recognised good practice
- internal audit work
- examining the results or outcomes of an activity.

The 3Es

- Economy – an input measure. Are the resources the cheapest possible for the quality desired?
- Efficiency – is the maximum output being acheived from the resources used?
- Effectiveness – are objectives being met?

Appropriate performance measures should be chosen for each 'E'.

The use of league tables (benchmarking) in the public sector

League tables have become increasingly popular in the public sector in recent years.

They are used to compare one organisation with another by ranking them in order of ability or achievement.

Advantages	Disadvantages
• Stimulates competition and the adoption of best practice.	• Input data may be poor.
	• Outcomes valued by society may be ignored if they are not measurable.
• Monitors and ensures accountability of providers.	• Encourages providers to focus on performance measures rather than the quality of the service.
• Performance is transparent.	• May encourage creative accounting.
	• Differences between providers may make comparisons meaningless.
• League tables should be readily available and can be used by consumers to make choices.	• A low ranking may have a negative impact on public trust and employee morale.
	• A low ranking could lead to a worsening of the future performance.

Benchmarking will be used to rank the organisation in the league table.

A **performance target** represents the level of performance that the organisation aims to achieve for a particular activity. Such targets should be SMART.

SPECIFIC, MEASURABLE, ACHEIVABLE, RELEVANT, TIME BOUND

Conflicts between targets	Central control by government	Difficulty level not right

Gaming i.e. play the system rather than using targets to improve performance

Issues with public sector targets

Not meeting the target seen as failure even if aspirational targets are set

Lack of ownership of targets

Targets not always appropriate e.g. lack of control by person responsible for achieving target

Cost may outweigh benefit

Too many targets

Exam sitting	Area examined	Question number	Number of marks
December 2014	VFM and performance indicators	2(b)	12
December 2013	League tables	4	25
June 2012	Public sector benchmarking	4	17
June 2010	VFM and the 3Es	3(i)(ii)	12
June 2009	Assessment of performance in a NFPO	1(a)	20
December 2008	League tables	1(b)	6
December 2007	Problems encountered when comparing public and private sector performance and VFM	1(b)(c)	12

11

Non-financial performance indicators

In this chapter

- Drawbacks of sole reliance on financial performance measures.
- Non-financial performance indicators.
- Models for evaluating financial and non-financial performance.

In order to fully appraise the performance of an organisation, it is useful to use a range of financial and non-financial performance indicators.

Drawbacks of sole reliance on financial performance measures`

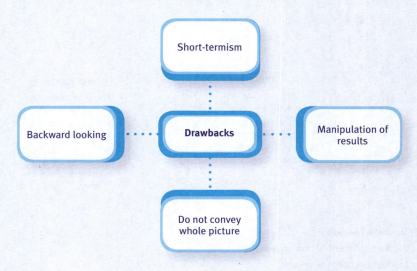

Non-financial performance indicators (NFPIs)

ADVANTAGES

- Easy to calculate
- Provided quickly
- Understood by non financial people
- Less likely to be manipulated

DISADVANTAGES

- Financial aspect cannot be ignored
- Possible information overload
- Pursuit of operational goals may blind managers to overall strategy

NFPIs play a key role in:

- the management of human resources
- product and service quality
- brand awareness and company profile.

KAPLAN PUBLISHING

Models for evaluating financial and non-financial performance

A number of models have been developed to facilitate a broader approach to measuring performance and the identification of a comprehensive range of measures. These look at different perspectives of performance and both financial and non-financial issues.

The balanced scorecard

- Translates an organisation's vision and strategy into objectives and measures
- Depends on the identification of strategic factors which determine the long-term future of the business.
- Based on four perspectives of performance.
- Was developed in 1992 by Kaplan and Norton.

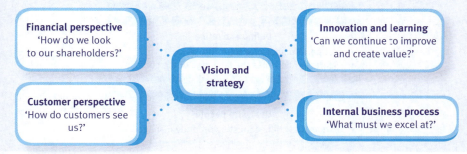

Financial perspective
'How do we look to our shareholders?'

Customer perspective
'How do customers see us?'

Vision and strategy

Innovation and learning
'Can we continue to improve and create value?'

Internal business process
'What must we excel at?'

Implementing the balanced sco

Make the strategy explicit
- Strategy forms the basis of the scorecard.
- May involve strategy mapping.

Choose the measures
- Align measures with strategy.
- Relationships between measures must be clearly understood.

Define and refine
- Put performance measures into place.
- Scorecard becomes the language of the company.

Deal with people
- People and change must be properly managed.

Advantages of balanced scorecard	Disadvantages of balanced scorecard
• Includes a mix of financial and non-financial measures. • Covers internal and external matters. • Links achievement of long-term and short-term objectives to achievement of strategy and vision.	• Difficult to record and process qualitative data. • Information overload. • Conflict between measures. • Measures may not align with strategy or vision. • Focuses on strategic level. • Lack of commitment by senior management. • Poor communication to employees and manager.

Fitzgerald's and Moon's building block

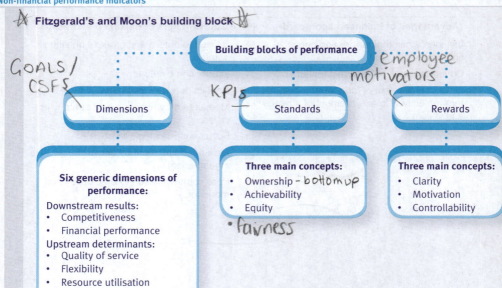

Building blocks of performance

GOALS / CSFS

KPIs

employee motivators

Dimensions

Standards

Rewards

Six generic dimensions of performance:

Downstream results:
- Competitiveness
- Financial performance

Upstream determinants:
- Quality of service
- Flexibility
- Resource utilisation
- Innovation

Three main concepts:
- Ownership – bottom up
- Achievability
- Equity

· fairness

Three main concepts:
- Clarity
- Motivation
- Controllability

124

Advantages of building block model	Disadvantages of building block model
• Includes financial and non-financial measures.	• Unsuitable for non-service companies.
• Tailored for service industry.	• Difficult to see how building blocks link to strategic objectives.
• Reward system should optimally motivate staff.	
• Targets are set in such a way to engage and motivate staff.	

The performance pyramid (Lynch and Cross)

- Defines the links between objectives and performance measures at different levels in the organisation.
- Designed to ensure that activities of every department, system and business unit support the overall organisational vision.

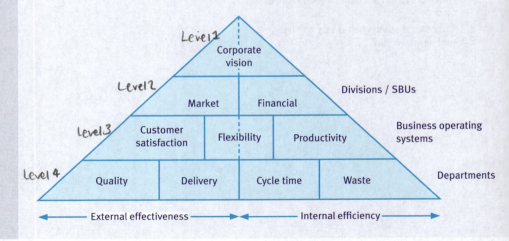

Advantages of performance pyramid	Disadvantages of performance pyramid
• Links performance measures at different levels of the organisation.	• Implementation uses management time and resource.
• Makes clear measures that are of interest to external parties and those that focus on internal factors.	• Some measures may conflict.

Exam sitting	Area examined	Question number	Number of marks
Sept/Dec 2015	Balanced scorecard	4	25
June 2015	Balanced scorecard	3(a), (b)	16
December 2014	NFPIs in the public sector	2(a)	6
December 2013	Performance pyramid	2(a)	15
June 2013	Balanced scorecard and building block model	1(iii)(iv)(v)	33
December 2011	Performance pyramid	2(b)(c)	18
June 2011	Building block model	3	20
June 2011	Balanced scorecard	2(a)(b)(d)	21
June 2010	NFPIs and the balanced scorecard	1(i)	13
June 2010	Performance pyramid	5(b)	12
December 2009	Assessment of financial and non-financial performance	1(ii)	10
June 2009	Balanced scorecard	1	35
June 2009	Drawbacks of sole reliance on financial performance measures	2(c)	6

December 2008	Evaluation of performance including building block model	1(a)	29
December 2007	Indicators of corporate failure	5(b)	10
Pilot paper	Assessment of financial performance and performance pyramid	2	25

12

Corporate failure

In this chapter

- Why do companies fail?
- Symptoms of failure.
- Corporate failure prediction models.
- Performance improvement strategies.
- The performance management system.
- Long-term survival and the product life-cycle.

Exam focus

So far we have focused on how effective performance management and measurement can help an organisation in achieving its goals. However, not all businesses will achieve their goals successfully. If left unchecked these businesses are at risk of corporate failure.

Why do companies fail?

There are many reasons why companies fail.

Strategic drift
The slow, incremental emergence of strategy when radical change demanded by environment

Poor management
- Marketing
- Quality
- Acquisitions

Inability to raise sufficient funds

Corporate failure
Company unable to achieve satisfactory return over the long-term

Failure of large project

Failure to adapt
(to changes in the environment)

Symptoms of failure

There are two main groups of symptoms:

| **Qualitative** | • information in the Chairman's or director's report
• information in the press
• information about environmental or external matters such as changes in the market |

| **Quantitative** | • problems with key liquidity, gearing and profitability ratios
• other problems in the published accounts such as a worsening cash position or large increases in intangible fixed assets |

Corporate failure prediction models

Altman's Z score

A quantitative model. The Z score is a ratio devised by Robert Altman to describe the financial health of a company, and its likelihood of financial distress.

Z score = $1.2X_1 + 1.4X_2 + 3.3X_3 + 0.6X_4 + 1.0X_5$

Where:

X_1 = working capital/total assets (liquidity)

X_2 = retained earnings/total assets (gearing)

X_3 = earnings before interest and tax/total assets (productivity of assets)

X_4 = market value of equity/total liabilities (equity decline before insolvency)

X_5 = sales/total assets (ability of assets to generate revenue)

Score:

- Less than 1.81 – company may be heading towards bankruptcy
- Between 1.81 and 2.99 – company needs further investigation to assess probability of failure
- 3 or above – company financially sound and expected to survive

↳ likely to fail within a 2 year period

✓ - calculations are simple

✓ - objective

✗ - bad score doesn't guarantee failure

✗ - may not be relevant to industry

✗ - further analysis needed to fully understand situation

Argenti's A score Overall score >25 = cause for concern

An example of a qualitative model. Relies on subjective scores to certain questions given by the investigator.

10/45 = X

- Defects – management weakness and accounting deficiencies may be included.
- Mistakes – occur as a result of defects and include high gearing, overtrading or failure of a big project. 15/45 = X
- Symptoms of failure – bleak financial indicators, creative accounting or non-financial signs such as high staff turnover.

	Quantitative models	Qualitative models

Features	• Incorporate trend analysis.
	• Take account of variations by industry.
	• Many models include a range of different variables:
	  – macroeconomic
	  – the quality of management
	  – the growth phase
	  – the quality of the company's assets.
		• May use information technology and systems such as expert systems.
		• Use is made of sets of rules based on the attributes of failing firms.
		• Systems have been developed which are capable of handling multiple criteria.

Limitations	• The score estimated is a snapshot. • Further analysis is needed to fully understand. • Scores are only good predictors in the short term. • Some scoring systems tend to rate companies low – that is they are likely to classify distressed firms as actually failing.	• Results only as good as the information which is input to them. • Based on the subjective judgement of experts.

Performance improvement strategies

Depends on spotting warning signs and taking quick corrective action.

• Accept that there is a problem and move on to a solution.

• May involve major strategic change.

• Put in controls to prevent further loss.

• Acquiring or developing new businesses (if resources allow) to spread the risk.

• Ensuring different parts of the business are in different stages of the life cycle.

• Learning from mistakes by performing due diligence ahead of an investment.

• Managing major risks such as fluctuations in commodity prices.

The performance management system

The performance management system will need to reflect the performance improvement strategies:

- Establish a link between new strategic goals and CSFs/KPIs.
- Set performance targets at all levels relating to the achievement of strategic objectives.
- Continuous review of actual performance against target.
- Address additional training/ development needs.

Long-term survival and the product life-cycle

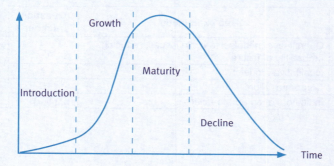

Long-term survival necessitates consideration of life-cycle issues:

Issue 1: there will be different CSFs (and hence KPIs) at different stages in the life-cycle

Issue 2: the stages of the life-cycle have different intrinsic levels of risk which should be understood and responded to.

It will be the scale of the financial resources which the organisation call on over the life of its products which will dictate its survival.

Exam sitting	Area examined	Question number	Number of marks
December 2014	Quantitative models, life-cycle issues, reducing probability of failure	4	20
December 2012	Qualitative models	4	11
December 2010	Corporate failure	5	15
December 2007	Indicators of corporate failure	5(b)	10

13

The role of quality in performance management

In this chapter

- Definitions.
- Quality-related costs.
- Quality practices.
- Lean production.
- Quality in management information systems.

In today's competitive global business environment, quality is one of the key ways in which a business can differentiate its product or service, improve performance and gain competitive advantage. Quality can form a key part of strategy.

Definitions

- **Quality** can be defined in a number of ways:
  - Is the product/service free from errors and does it adhere to design specifications?
  - Is the product fit for service/use?
  - Does the product/service meet customers' needs?
- **Quality management** involves planning and controlling activities to ensure the product or service is fit for purpose, meets design specifications and meets the needs of the customers.
- **Quality control** involves a number of routine steps which measure and control the quality of the product/service as it is developed.
- **Quality assurance** involves a review of quality control procedures to verify the desired level of quality has been met. The review is usually carried out by an independent body such as ISO (see below).
- The **International Organisation for Standardisation (ISO)** is one of the major bodies responsible for producing quality standards. Companies seeking ISO registration must fulfil certain criteria.
- A **quality management system** is a set of co-ordinated activities to direct and control an organisation in order to continually improve its performance.

Quality-related costs

Monitoring the costs of quality is key to the operation of any quality improvement programme.

The organisation's costing system should be capable of identifying and collecting these costs.

Quality practices

Kaizen costing

Definition

Kaizen costing focuses on producing small, incremental cost reductions throughout the production process through the products life.

Steps:

1 During the design phase, a target cost is set for each production function.

2 The target costs are totalled to give a baseline target cost for the product's first year of production.

3 As the process improves, cost reductions reduce the baseline cost.

4 Cost reduction targets are set on a regular basis and variance analysis is carried out.

Total quality management (TQM)

- Prevention of errors before they occur
- Real participation by all
- **Features**
- Management commitment
- Continual improvement

Just-in-time

Definition

Just-in-time (JIT) is a system whose objective is to produce or procure products or components as they are required rather than for inventory.

Requirements:

- High quality and reliability.
- Elimination of non-value added activities.
- Speed of throughput to match demand.
- Flexibility.
- Lower costs.

BENEFITS:
- INCREASED CUSTOMER FOCUS
- BUSINESS PROCESS IMPROVEMENTS
- DECISION MAKING DRIVEN BY DATA / FACTS
- PROACTIVE MANAGEMENT INVOLVEMENT
- WHOLE ORGANISATION FOCUS ON QUALITY ISSUES

Step 3: **A**nalyse the opportunity
ROOT CAUSE OF ISSUES

Step 4: **I**mprove performance
DEVELOP SOLUTIONS

Step 5: **C**ontrol performance
ACTUAL VS TARGET

Lean production

Definition

Lean production is a philosophy of management based on cutting out waste and unnecessary activities including:

- Over-production
- Inventory
- Waiting
- Defective units
- Motion
- Transportation
- Over-processing

In terms of a **MIS**, a lean approach would aim to eliminate waste and improve the efficiency and flow of information to users.

The **five Ss** concept is often associated with lean principles and has the aim of creating a workplace which is in order.

Structurise: eg) optimal locations for storage

Systemise: arrange items for ease of use and approach tasks systematically

Sanitise: avoid clutter

Standardise: be consistent in the approach taken

Self discipline: Sustain – do the above daily.

Quality in management information systems

Four features of a quality system

Fuctionality
- system perfoms tasks it was designed for

Reliability
- system not susceptible to downtime and outputs are accurate and complete

Usability
- system is user friendly

Build quality
- e.g. ease of maintenance and upgrade

Exam sitting	Area examined	Question number	Number of marks
Sept/Dec 2015	DMAIC	3(a)	15
December 2013	Lean management and accountability	3(b)(c)	13
June 2012	Six Sigma	3	17
December 2011	Quality costs, Kaizen and JIT	5	20
June 2010	Cost targets and quality costs	5(a)	8
June 2009	Six Sigma	5	20
December 2008	Software quality and service quality	2(c)(d)	7
December 2008	Quality costs	4(b)	8
June 2008	Quality costs and elimination of quality problems	5	20
Pilot paper	Service quality	1(e)	6

14

Environmental management accounting

In this chapter

- Drawbacks of traditional management accounting.
- Using EMA to address these problems.
- EMA techniques.

Exam focus

Organisations are becoming increasingly aware of the environmental implications of their actions.

Drawbacks of traditional management accounting

Traditional management accounting systems are unable to adequately deal with environmental costs:

Type of environmental cost	Problem
Conventional costs, e.g. energy costs.	Not prioritised since often hidden in overheads.
Contingent costs, e.g. decommissioning costs.	Often ignored due to short-term focus.
Relationship costs, e.g. cost of producing environmental information for reporting.	Ignored by managers who may be unaware of their existence.
Reputational cost, i.e. the cost of failing to address environmental issues.	Ignored by managers who are unaware of the risk of incurring them.

Using EMA to address these problems

Benchmarking activities against environmental best practice

Include environment - related indicators as part of performance monitoring

Assess the likelihood and impact of environmental risks

AIMS OF EMA

Identify and estimate the costs of environment – related activities

Identify and monitor the usage of resources

Ensure environmental considerations form part of capital investment appraisal

EMA techniques

There are two main techniques:

| ABC | • Removes environment-driven costs from overheads and traces them to products or services. |
| | • Should result in the identification of cost drivers and better control of costs. |

| Lifecycle costing | • Considers the costs and revenues of a product over its whole life rather than one accounting period. |
| | • In order to reduce lifecycle costs may use techniques such as TQM. |

Exam sitting	Area examined	Question number	Number of marks
December 2014	EMA	3	25
June 2011	EMA	5	20
December 2010	Environmental performance	4	20

Index

KAPLAN PUBLISHING